REFLECTIONS

A catalogue record of this book is available from the British Library

First Edition: November 2006

ISBN: 1-84375-250-6

To order additional copies of this book please visit:
http://www.upso.co.uk/barbaraliddle

Published by: UPSO Ltd
5 Stirling Road, Castleham Business Park,
St Leonards-on-Sea, East Sussex TN38 9NW United Kingdom
Tel: 01424 853349 Fax: 0870 191 3991
Email: info@upso.co.uk Web: http://www.upso.co.uk

REFLECTIONS

by

Barbara Liddle

UPSO

This book is dedicated to the memory of my father, who instilled in me during my schooldays an abiding love of the English language, and to my first husband, John Larkin, who always set himself seemingly impossible goals – but achieved them. I am deeply grateful for the affectionate support and encouragement of all my children over the years. It is as a result of their faith in me and the gentle persuasion of my many friends that this collection of poetry has finally been published.

An extra thank you goes to my No. 2 son, Shaun Larkin for his perfect illustrations.

CONTENTS PAGE

JANUARY

Interface. 3
The Beautiful People 4
My Father 6
The Legacy. 7
This Time, Next Time 8
Waiting 9

FEBRUARY

Shopping for a Poem 13
Faces at an Exhibition. 14
Cry from the Heart. 16
The Wall 18
Alien 20
Dawn Dreams 22
The Yoga Class 24
Ode to Bristles 26

MARCH

Dance of Life 31
True Love. 32
The Gravedigger. 34
The Shoe 35
Baby 36
Fishing. 37
Transport of Delight. 38

APRIL

Response to Spring 43
The Silence of Eternity 44
The Silence of Eternity (2) 45
A Woman in my own Right 46
Limericks 48
Shorelines – Quatrain Practice 50

MAY

Lena's Garden 55
Dead Flowers 56
The Years Between 57
Living with Epilepsy 58
For Steven 60
The Honour of the Game 61
The BT Man 64

JUNE

Siesta 69
Time Trap 70
House-hunting 72
Poverty 74
Truth 75
Wildfire 76
A Time and Place 77

JULY

Crete 81
The Swimming Pool 82
The Natchez Trace 84
After Puglia 85
Malta 86
Tuscan Holiday 88
Calvi in Corsica 89
Tunisia 90
Vacances à Montagny 91

AUGUST

Martha's Kitchen 95
Houses 96
Shadows 98
Earth 99
Love Life of a Temp 100
The Colour of Hope 102
Metamorphosis of Emily 103

SEPTEMBER

Dreams of Dragons 107
St Andrew's Church 108
Frustrated Muse 110
Frustrated Muse (2) 111
Tides 112
Neighbours 114
Agony Aunts 115

OCTOBER

Deserted Cottage 119
Stillborn 120
The Buchan Ball 121
Wedding Day 124
The Amateur Photographer 127
Sunset 128

NOVEMBER

Ruth 133
The Grey Ones 134
Computer Blues 136
Change of Address 138
A Pill for all Seasons 139
Don't Make Me Promises 140

DECEMBER

The Christmas List 145
Aftermath 147
Resurrection 148
Birds in Winter 149
Love in a Cold Climate 150
Windows in Winter 151
Thoughts 152

January

INTERFACE

Small but all-embracing screen, patterned in black and
    luminescent green;
There is no sound, but yet your voiceless signals tell me much.
My finger's slightest touch erases or creates;
At my command the cursor moves – it has no will
    save that which I instil.
Ideas inchoate, unrefined – dredged from the hidden depths
    within my mind
And, faster than the speed of light,
Translated from the abstract into electronic byte.
Black box wizardry, micro-chip imagery;
This is the interface between, here on the screen.
Poetic fancy and technology conjoined in mystic consummation.

Cut and copy, paste, delete, to make the final version neat.
No-one will ever see the variations on a theme;
Half-written lines that didn't scan,
A verse that didn't match the plan I thought I had conceived.
Errors erased so fast it's hard to realise that they had ever been;
Consigned to limbo, not in my memory but the machine's.
Is human inspiration magnified or stultified by such complexity?
It vexes me not to know.

Can I, can anyone, believe the painful striving for perfection,
When nothing but the final version's left to print?
The cursor blinks at me accusingly and does not move;
We are both poised and waiting, caught in a bubble of time;
Waiting for something undefined – a word, a thought, a rhyme?
This is the interface between, here on the screen.
Computerised composition, patterned in black and luminescent
    green.

THE BEAUTIFUL PEOPLE

Have you noticed how the people in the TV soaps are all the same?
The women are all young and slim and tanned.
There isn't one who hasn't got a man in tow,
Or maybe two or three!
There isn't one who looks like *me.*

The men are tall and handsome too, with perfect teeth.
Muscled and bronzed, they still have hair.
It may be dark or blonde, distinguished grey –
But it's still there!
Sometimes the bad guys are charming too;
None of the good guys looks like *you.*

They all drive cars like limousines;
Not a scratch, a trace of mud, a dented wing
To show you where they've been.
Even the garage is the size of Carnegie Hall;
The people in the TV soaps never use a bus at all!
And have you ever noticed, when they drive from A to B,
They can always park *exactly* where it is they have to be.

And when the lovely people meet to dine
Discreetly over steak chasseur and wine,
The waiters always hover, the chairs are nicely placed;
No-one says "You should have booked before."
Or puts *them* at a table by the door.
Every image oozes nonchalant good taste.

Reflections

In bedroom scenes – and there's always lots of those,
Naked people lie between designer sheets.
Only fuddy-duddies wear pyjamas
Or bedsocks on their frozen feet!
Ladies rise from beds of lust, their hairstyle still in place.
I cannot manage that – there's always a trace
Of passion left within my heart, upon my face.

I know they're meant to be glossy, the TV soaps.
Escapism, that's what they are,
But I'm sick of synthetic people with plastic smiles
Living their celluloid lives in immaculate style.
I wish that sometimes, just sometimes on TV,
The 'beautiful people' would look and live and love
Like you and me!

Barbara Liddle

MY FATHER

They say that every father casts a shadow,
Touching lives that owe their spark to him;
Spiritual umbilical, never cut completely,
Though time or distance make our memories dim.
My father was a short and round and gentle man;
A hint of fine, fair hair upon a balding head,
His blue eyes guileless as a summer sky.
I loved him with a fierce, abiding love
That stayed with me long after he was dead.
In homespun habit, simple sandals on his feet,
He would have been a Friar Tuckish kind of guy;
He was a fan of Robin Hood – and so was I.
His photograph still hangs upon the wall;
The box he carved within a German prison camp
Still sits upon the table in the hall.

THE LEGACY

The book was lying hidden,
Long-forgotten in a bureau drawer;
A map of Deutschland on the inside cover at the back
And on the front a soldier's name and rank and regiment.
On yellowing paper words lay neatly spaced upon the page,
In serried rows, like soldiers on parade.
It was a serving soldier who had set them there long years ago,
A prisoner in a barbed wire cage;
His dreams of home and freedom given form and shape
In these few poems in a well-thumbed book.
He was an artist too, this prisoner-of-war;
Some sketches done in pen and ink showed promise of a talent
there,
But yet the tranquil sylvan scenes showed sentry boxes 'mid the
trees
And tiny numbers showed a date
That fell before the Armistice was signed.
Ninety years ago a young man sat with captive friends
And penned the letters sent to parents far away.
In text-book shorthand, faded strokes record the gist of what he
said
While extracts from his diary tell of weary hours
And Red Cross parcels,
Of endless cabbage soup and fretting youth.
Such are the fragments of a life that's gone,
But nothing is wasted, nothing lost.
This is the legacy my father gave to me,
And so, today, I write and dream and hope, as he did then;
Though not a prisoner I,
And free to do whate'er I will,
In me his poet's soul lives still.

Barbara Liddle

THIS TIME, NEXT TIME

Next time around I'll stop and look at things a little longer,
Take time to smell each garden flower;
Take time to listen to the birdsong,
To savour all the sweetness of each hour.

Next time around I'll go a little slower with romance,
Take time to let him know I care;
Take time to memorise each facet of his face,
To treasure all the moments that we share.

Next time around I'll be a little kinder to myself,
Take time to know the person that I am;
Take time to think about directions,
Where I'm going, what I'm doing, while I can.

This time around I've moved too fast with everything;
Afraid of wasting time, I've been too prodigal
With what I had or where I've been.
Striving to reach the signposts up ahead,
Ignoring all the loveliness of places in between.

Next time around I'll use my life more wisely,
Next time around I won't make these mistakes again.
Maybe those things promised for the next time
Should be practised now, not then;
Maybe I should stop and savour this time
For it may not come again.

WAITING

My tiny world is dark, I cannot see
Although my eyes are beautifully formed,
And fringed lashes lie upon my virgin cheek.
Floating in warmth, I flex my limbs
And punch my flailing fists into
The soft, constraining limits of my living tomb;
Growing in strength, soon to begin the journey of my life
Outside the womb.
My movements are restricted in this confined space;
And though I feel the life-beat, hear the voices close,
I've not yet looked upon a human face.
Strange to consider that my life began before my birth;
Technology has told my mother that she bears a son
But I, dependent on her for my every need,
Know nothing of her yet –
Save that she cares for me.
Both of us waiting, waiting, wearily now,
For that sweet moment when we meet at last;
Free of my cushioning prison, yet held fast
In arms that form a cradle for my tiny frame,
While that same voice I've heard before
Sighs with contentment at a job well done,
And softly murmurs to her sleeping son his name.

February

SHOPPING FOR A POEM

I dreamt last night there was a shop
Where you could buy a poem off the shelf;
One that was bespoke, that you could call your own;
One that you didn't have to write yourself
Or finely tune, and hone.
It was a kind of DIY store, a writer's B & Q;
Words of every size and shape, meanings of every hue;
And sections stocking metaphors, or jumbo packs of rhyme.
All the tools of the writer's trade, to save the poet time.
Bright ideas in polythene bags, two for the price of one;
Imagination in a coloured box – though all the stocks were gone!
But poetry doesn't come 'flat-packed',
It can't be 'assembled' just like that.
It doesn't have a book of instructions, telling you what to do;
It comes from inspiration, it has to come from YOU.
So I'm glad that my dream was only a dream,
For poems aren't born on a shelf.
They live in the heart of a poet;
I'd much rather write one myself.

Barbara Liddle

FACES AT AN EXHIBITION

People at an exhibition.
Preview for invited guests on opening night;
Free wine and free admission.
The pictures on the wall are unequivocally
Black and white.
Photographic studies of mankind;
The artist is well-known – elsewhere,
By some.
The gathered people in the gallery are,
For the most part, unaware.
To be seen, not to see, is why they're there,
The only reason why they've come.

The faces on the wall look down and wonder why
They are so often gazed at with unseeing eyes.
The glossy catalogues are there with names
For all the numbered portraits in their frames,
But no-one reads them, no-one knows,
The viewers or the viewed,
Whose faces are the ones on show.

Here is an old man, shoulders drooping with despair;
See how a streak of sunlight sets aglow his silver hair.
And this face here, this is the face of innocence –
Her dreams are still intact;
Stark contrast to the ragged children,
Faces older than their years,
Who stare behind barbed wire.
Can you not feel the weight of all their unshed tears?
Mother and baby, study in gentleness;
Unemployed vagrant, picture of hopelessness.

Reflections

Why have they bothered coming here at all,
These people with their backs towards the wall?
Sipping their wine and laughing too loudly,
They are not looking at the portraits on display.
They barely know the artist or his work at all;
Would they have come if they had had to pay?
Their empty faces simply don't compare
With those that are already there
Upon the wall.

Suppose the viewers and the viewed reversed their roles,
Perhaps the portrait people would not look at *them;*
Or else dismiss with glancing recognition –
They are just faces at an exhibition.

CRY FROM THE HEART!

I'm depressed – again!
It's the third time this week.
My diet isn't working, my new shoes have a squeak.
The weather's been fine and sunny,
So you'd think I'd be happy with that;
But it made all my butter go runny,
And doubled the fleas on the cat!
And everyone else has a glorious tan
While I'm turning patchy and red;
My expensive perm? – well, it just didn't take –
There isn't a curl on my head!

My favourite dress went and shrank in the wash,
There's a new little scratch on my car.
I'm lonely and fat – I eat 'cos of that,
So I just make things worse than they are.
Nobody phoned me again today;
I think my new answerphone scares them away.
There are ants in the back yard, the loo is erratic;
I've jiggled the ballcock like some plumbing fanatic
But sometimes it works and sometimes it don't;
It flows when it wants to but sometimes it won't.
My African violet's looking sick, my horoscope's no good,
And I've found some telltale wormholes in a lovely bit of wood.
I bought myself a magazine, an article on stress –
It seems that I'm a classic case, no wonder I'm depressed!

Reflections

If you've got it, depression's a terrible thing,
Spiralling down to the depths of despair,
Climbing back out an impossible task
When nobody seems to care.
I need someone to tell me I am statuesque – not fat;
I need someone to fix the loo, someone to cure the cat.
I need someone to lean on, just while I'm feeling blue;
Everyone needs somebody, and right now I need you.
When you're low and you really need someone,
Someone who'll show that they care –
That's when it's **really** depressing –
To know that there's nobody there!

Barbara Liddle

THE WALL

Obscene structure of stone and wire,
Immovable, implacable, focus of hatred and despair;
Symbol of division, West and East,
Beauty and Beast – but which is which?

Megalith, man-made, subservient to none,
Slogans inscribed in letters three feet high.
Some come to look and photograph, but do not heed;
The silent stones drown out the human cry.

Man has built walls before;
Some, as in China, standing still.
Miracles of construction,
A thousand, thousand beads of sweat,
Bent backs of human beasts of burden
Have blended with the builder's skill
To leave a monument to man's insatiable desire
For self-protection.

Touch, in Jerusalem, the Wailing Wall,
Where pain and prayer mingle,
Binding the stones together with tenacious faith.
Stand upon Hadrian's Wall,
And look into the distant green;
Feel the chill north winds upon your cheek
And pity those who came before,
When stones were newly placed and roofs were raised
To keep the hostile elements at bay.

Reflections

Castles or cottages, prisons or palaces,
Man cannot live without his walls;
But this one wall should never have been built at all.
Obscene structure of stone and wire,
Immovable, implacable, focus of hatred and despair;
Symbol of division, East and West;
Who can guess when you will fall?

This was written in May, 1989 and only a few weeks later the Berlin Wall began to be dismantled, and East and West mingled freely.

Barbara Liddle

ALIEN

Alien, you are not welcome here;
We know from whence you come
And why you journeyed into Space.
You are not welcome here,
We know about the human race.
You had a planet once where man could live in harmony
But you destroyed it
Piece by piece and bit by bit
Till there was nothing left of it.
Extinction was your natural end.

We watched you as you played your games
Of international bargaining.
We noted names
Of leaders who corrupted and, in turn, became corruptible.
Though they began their task with ideals good and hopes so
    high,
They all became world-weary, disillusioned
And, ultimately, ceased to try.
You were like children squabbling over toys;
Fair weather friends, concerned with self-aggrandisement.

And not one thought about the future of mankind;
You reckoned it a million miles away.
In different corners of the Earth
Your power became the means of self-destruction.
In every language, talk just heightened indecision;
And suddenly you felt the chilling touch of world despair,
The moon's dark side for ever.
You realized the Future was Today,
And there was nowhere safe to run away.

Reflections

You turned your eyes away from Earth and thought
With vandal hearts and greedy grasp to plunder Space;
But you're not welcome here,
You remnants of the human race.
Go back from whence you came;
Re-build the shattered fragments of your lives,
Your planet Earth,
And learn from past mistakes
That something precious, fragile,
Left in careless hands,
Will always break.

Barbara Liddle

DAWN DREAMS

'Tis Dawn and I, alas, Awake;
My Love beside me, still she sleeps
And snores! – until the Couch whereon I lie
Begins to shake.

Where now the Langurous Limbs and Perfum'd Breasts
That once a young man's blood enflam'd?
The eyes of Love see none too clear;
Where now the Heavenly Houri once I claim'd?

Full score and more the years have flown;
The Honey'd Tongue which once dripp'd Loving Words
Dost now accost mine ear with shrill and bitter nagging,
Pecking away like Ravening Birds.

Oh, to be rid of her; bid her be Gone.
The Moon of my Delight hath wax'd and waned
So oft she is become a Burden Sore;
The Balm of Marriage Bed thrice turn'd a Bane.

But how be free of her? How to contrive?
In Truth, interment while she's still Alive
Is hardly fitting, Unworthy of my erstwhile Vows.
A funeral pyre creates pollution;
It doesn't seem a good solution.
Set her afloat in a Waterproof Box,
In a Waterproof Shroud and Waterproof Socks?
Sufficient water's hard to find;
And not dead yet – it seems Unkind.
I must think of Something – Oh, let it be Soon;
Could I fill her full of helium, and fly her to the Moon?

'Tis Dawn and I, alas, Awake;
Such dreams I banish – they are not to be;
My Love beside me, still she sleeps,
And dreams, perhaps, how to be rid of me.

Barbara Liddle

THE YOGA CLASS

Discard your clumpy shoes and heavy winter coat;
Squeeze into your leotard, pull on your woolly socks.
Here is where your body becomes obedient to your mind.
Find a space and spread your mat upon the floor;
Stand tall and let your toes relax,
Lose the tension in each muscle,
Leave the world outside, outside.

Slowly bending, slowly stretching
To the rhythm of your breathing;
Like a tree, on one foot balanced,
Raise your arms and hold the pose.
Now the Lotus, keep the focus,
Let your thoughts escape the treadmill,
Daily treadmill of your mind,
Leave the world outside, outside.

Now's the time for relaxation,
Lying inert upon your mat.
Savasanna, floating, floating;
Feel the lightness, the space inside.
Hold awareness while unwinding,
Concentrate on meditation,
Heart and pulse rate calming, calming,
Leave the world outside, outside.

Reflections

This is not the time for sleeping,
You are always in control;
Totally at ease with your whole being
The big reward is levitation.
Do not lose your concentration
Or the magic disappears.
All too soon the class is ending,
Summoned by the world outside, outside.

ODE TO BRISTLES

Some women long for diamonds,
Some women yearn for pearls;
But I just want a bristle brush –
I'm not like other girls!

I do the weekly cleaning,
And I like to do my best
With 'Henry', mop and duster,
But corners were a pest.

A bristle brush was needed
For the bits that 'Henry' missed;
A soft brush couldn't do the job,
On real bristles I'd insist.

When I saw them in my hardware store
My heart just leapt with joy;
And now my lovely bristle brush
Is just my favourite toy!

In all the nooks and crannies
Where the crumbs stick to the floor
I can reach them with my bristles –
So much cleaner then before.

You can keep your plastic brushes
With their bristles dyed bright blue;
This old-fashioned girl loves bristles,
Brown and boring, but reliable and true!

March

DANCE OF LIFE

From my eyes a thousand tears have welled,
But nothing's changed.
Immutable, the source of envy or of grief.
A thousand useless battles have I waged
And nothing gained;
Shaken and crushed my spirit and belief.
If, then, the world outside I cannot change,
It must be *me* who yields in strife
And learns surrender to the Dance of Life.

Barbara Liddle

TRUE LOVE

There's a poggle in my pond
And he's eaten all my fish;
And I didn't put them in there
To provide a tasty dish
For a poggle that is fatter
Than a poggle ought to be.
A poggle's tummy wobble
Is a sorry sight to see.

It's unhealthy for a poggle
To be grossly overweight,
And it sets a bad example
To the fribble by the gate.
Yes, I've got a little fribble
In the rosebed by the gate;
She's a lonely little fribble
'cos she hasn't got a mate;
Though I've tried to find her someone
Compatible and kind,
An eligible fribble
Is impossible to find.

There's a lecherous old sleazle
Who fancies her a lot;
He lurks in next door's garden
Drinking vodka, smoking pot!
But my lonely little fribble
For such a weasel would not fall;
She has yearnings for the poggle,
Who doesn't notice her at all.

But true love will find a way, they say,
And much to my surprise
It was the treacherous sleazle
Who opened poggle's eyes.
For seduction of the fribble
The sleazle's scene was set
When suddenly the poggle
Shouted "Fribble, don't you fret!
We poggles may be portly
But we're fearless in a fight."
Forthwith he squashed the sleazle flat,
And kicked him out of sight.

The poggle and the fribble live together
In the arbour by the pond;
And I've planted roses round it
'cos of them the fribble's fond.
And she watches poggle's diet
To prevent him being obese.
It's a very happy ending
So I leave them both in peace.

Barbara Liddle

THE GRAVEDIGGER

I work in all weathers, rain or shine;
A solitary occupation, mine.
People walk past, they've nothing to say;
They don't even pass the time of day.
I 'spect they have other things on their minds;
It's a funny old world – it takes all kinds.

The Vicar, now, sometimes stops for a chat;
We often talk about this and that.
He sees things different – the big connection
Between life on earth and resurrection;
Between those that are damned and those that are saved,
But I don't believe in all that stuff – I just digs the grave.

Week after week I'm just digging the holes
For the mortal remains – I don't know about "souls".
But 'tis peaceful here in the old churchyard;
I likes the outdoors, though the digging is hard.
And I'm not as young as I used to be,
So my joints often ache; my back and my knees.
I've time to think about life after death,
If there is such a thing, when I've drawn my last breath.
If I do get to Heaven, though the chosen are few,
What's a poor fellow like me to do?
Life everlasting, 'n joy abundant;
A humble gravedigger is quite redundant!

THE SHOE

Did he know, that cobbler, long ago
His shoes would far outlast his mortal span?
Did his children watch, bewitched,
As he hammered, shaped, and stitched?
Did they realise the skill within his hands?
Dainty shoes were made of satin, pigskin or brocade,
Never meant to bear the brunt of common land;
But these of sturdy leather, to resist the winter weather,
These were shoes to serve a working man.
A yeoman's feet they shod;
Country paths they must have trod,
For the wearing shows in every crack and crease.
Of the pair there's only one;
No-one knows where t'other's gone,
And the humble wearer long since rests in peace.

*Written in September 2000, after a visit to Brian and Audrey's house
and being shown a wonderful old shoe found in their chimney.*

Barbara Liddle

BABY

Small fat baby with dark chocolate eyes
Sits in his bath and solemnly sucks the sponge;
Plump and round and pink,
With damp curls resting on his neck,
Wriggles his toes and ponders the mystery
Of slippery soapsuds escaping his baby grasp.

Small, fat baby, cocooned in fluffy towel,
Lies on his back and waves his arms
To catch the fragrant powder falling from above;
Swoons with delight as someone tickles his tum,
And wraps his tiny fingers round a giant's thumb.

Small, fat baby tucked up in bed,
Fights against drowsiness, kicks off the covers;
Upside-down baby, nappy-swathed bottom high in the air,
While ten little toes like a row of pink peas
Dare you to touch, disturbing his dreams.

Memories triggered off by my eldest son's 33rd birthday!

FISHING

Some days he just sits in his chair,
Staring out of the window;
Not really knowing where or who he is,
Not really caring any more.
His thoughts are drifting on a chartless sea;
A voyage without purpose to an unknown shore.
He's trawling his mind for memories,
Hauling in his catch,
Sighing when there's nothing there.

Some days are cruel;
Nothing to show for hours and hours
Of sweeping through the years,
Not even yesterday's small fry,
Yesterday's tears.

Some days are better,
Some days his nets are full
As memories spill over from the past,
Bright and shining,
Slippery as silver fish.

Barbara Liddle

TRANSPORT OF DELIGHT

I wander'd lonely as a cloud
That floats on high o'er hill and vale,
When all at once I saw a crowd,
A host of cars stuck nose to tail.
Beside the slip road, 'neath the trees,
All becalmed on tarmac seas.

Continuous headlights all did shine
and twinkle on the cat's eye'd main;
they stretch'd in never-ending line
from Junction 6 to Clacket Lane.
Three hundred saw I at a glance
revving their engines for advance.

Drivers behind the wheel did curse;
a tedious crawl each did essay.
O Death, what fate is worse
than tail-back on the motorway?
I gazed and gazed, but little thought
What joy the motor-car to me had brought.

For oft, when travelling homeward bound,
in vacant or in pensive mood,
the traffic to a halt has ground;
the air turns blue with language rude,
and then my heart is fill'd with pain
to think I could have gone by train.

April

RESPONSE TO SPRING

Pale primrose yellow yields to brass-bold gold of gorse
And skies are clearer now than then.
Massed bluebells shout their message of defiance to departing
   clouds
And streams reflect the leafy canopies above them in the glen.

Like pollen in the air, the smell of growth is all around;
Town gardens turn from brown to green,
And people, too, begin to shake the memory of winter from their
   minds
And walk with springier step into the summer scene.

This is the season of the paint-pot and the brush,
As walls and woodwork gleam 'neath busy hands.
Like blocks of icecream stand the houses tall,
A terrace full of sugared strands.

This is no time for sitting still in quiet reflection;
Nature responds with urgency to springtime sun,
And so should we.
This is the time for starting life anew,
For brightness and for change;
Shake off the shackles of dull habit and feel free.

THE SILENCE OF ETERNITY

Where are the silver trumpets?
The choirs of angelic hosts?
Don't Seraphim and Cherubim
Sing to the Holy Ghost?

Where are the Saints and Martyrs
Praising the Lord on high?
It seems to me that there ought to be
A lot of noise in the sky.

If, on the Day of Judgement,
The sheep, not the goats, are preferred,
There should be some sheepish rejoicing,
A glorious sound should be heard.

So where are the sounds of laughter?
Loved voices I long to hear?
The Silence of Eternity
Is not for me, I fear.

I'd like to be forgiven,
But I want someone to know;
If it's going to be silent in Heaven,
I'd rather stay Down Below!

THE SILENCE OF ETERNITY (2)

A million light years to a star;
The beauty of the Universe,
How far away it seems from daily life,
The bustle and the hurry and the strife.
My earthly world is noisy, full of sound;
I can't escape, it's all around me,
Every moment, every day.
Only in sleep it seems to go away.

Tiny sounds like the nibbling of mice,
Ominous sounds like the cracking of ice;
Fireworks, thunder, traffic's roar,
Shushing of ripples on shingle shore;
Angry winds and gentle breezes,
Sounds of laughter, coughs and sneezes.
Footsteps shuffling, running, walking
And hundreds of people just talking, talking!
Cars and lorries, trains and planes,
Rhythm of raindrops on wet window panes;
The rumble of landslide, the crackle of fire,
The crying of babies, harmonious choir;
Roadworks drilling, telephones shrilling,
Computers clicking, clocks a-ticking;
Even in Death
There's still the sound of one last breath.
So when I die, sing loud and long for me,
Make joyous noise, my friend.
I dread the silence of eternity –
It is too vast for me to comprehend.

Barbara Liddle

A WOMAN IN MY OWN RIGHT

I'm going to be assertive, from now on;
I've read a book about the ways that I am put upon.
I needn't be a doormat, so it says;
I have to learn to say just what I want.
I have to learn to **know** I have a choice,
I have to practise being a mouse that's **bold**,
And let the others round about me hear my voice.
Yes, being assertive's just the thing I need;
No-one appreciates a timorous, weak-willed weed.
It's only now I realize what I've done –
For years I've given in to father, husband, son!
It's time I took a stand and made it clear
The worm has turned;
Assertiveness is here, to stay – I hope.
The world will see a newer, brighter me
Once I have mastered this strange art, this new philosophy,
Which tells me I'm as good as all the rest.
I've equal rights to ask from life not second-best
But just exactly what I want.
Of course, I may not get what I expect, demand, deserve;
There's some will look at me askance and tell me I've a nerve
To speak up after all these years of giving in.
But I must learn to be a **person**, just like them
And set my self-assessment as la crème!
'Tis said the meek, one day, inherit all the earth,
but let me tell you, folks, for what it's worth,
I don't agree.

Reflections

There are no dividends in being meek that I can see!
Don't get me wrong, I'm not a feminist;
I'm not campaigning for equality or such;
In fact, I'm really not demanding much at all.
Mere recognition of **_my rights_**,
That I am just as good as men;
But, just before the new assertive me bursts forth
Upon an unsuspecting world,
Perhaps I'd better read the book again!!!

LIMERICKS

There once was a fellow called Adam!
Whose wife was an absolute Madam!
She led him astray
With an apple one day,
Just exactly what God had forbade 'em!

A lady who longed to lose weight
Cut by half everything that she ate.
Her diet so sparse
Reduced hips, thighs and arse!
So now she's a slender Size 8!!

An actor named Robert J. Heinz
Could never remember his lines.
He hadn't a clue
When given his cue,
But at dubbing cartoons he's just fine!

It isn't easy writing verse
And limericks are even worse
There's a definite beat and a definite rhyme
And you can't get it right just time after time.
In a wonderful line there's that fateful word
Whose only match is absurd – or purred!
So you start again with a bright idea
And once more you're stuck, I fear, oh dear.
A passionate plumber from Putney
Adored pickled onions and chutney;
His love of things spicy
Became rather pricey
So instead of prime lamb he ate mutt'ney!

Reflections

It's not so hard with verse that's free,
The words don't have to rhyme, you see,
So that's the style for me, for me –
Yes, that's the style for me!!!

SHORELINES (Quatrain practice)

The land here slips into the sea and disappears.
The slow tides lap and wrap themselves around,
Claiming another foot, another yard, another home
While puny man looks out across the waves – and loses ground.

Smooth as the rocks with clear pools enigmatically lying,
Smooth as the sand washed clean by slow receding tides,
Smooth as the air where seagulls celebrate their freedom, flying,
I wish the shoreline of my heart could know such peace.

Like metall'd moth I flew above
And watched the passionate embrace of shore and ocean.
Here, at the very edge of man's domain,
The foamflecked breakers in perpetual motion.

Do I face death or life upon this unknown shore?
Which, in my fragile state, do I fear more?
My heart beats stronger now, there is no turning back
Now is the moment when I claim new earth,
Re-incarnation in another birth.

A shoreline = a boundary between the known and unknown

May

LENA'S GARDEN

Hot and still, the drowsy garden dreams,
While in the undergrowth the midges dance in beams of sun.
Irridescent blue, a dragon-fly hovers over lily pool
And lazy fish swim languidly beneath its placid face.
A fine blue net protects them now from predatory heron,
And lush green plants surround this watery place.
The kitchen garden, fecund with summer fruits,
Is slowly being choked with rampant weeds.
An ancient Morris van lies rusting
In the unkempt grass beyond the lawn;
Bright yellow, like some giant larva of an alien breed.
Trees, especially sycamores, vie with each other
For light and space, as do the flowers.
Roses, heavy-headed, drooping in the heat;
Lavender, Sweet William, pale statue gleaming.
Nothing is neat or clipped, symmetrical,
But wanton, unexpected,
And everywhere the heady scent of green things growing.
A mighty scythe leans up against a wall;
And blonde, chopped wood, foretaste of winter fires,
Lies ready to be stacked beneath the house on stilts.
A robin perches on abandoned garden fork,
Scanning the fresh turned earth,
While nearby works the gardener, on her knees.
She knows that though she works from dawn to dusk
The garden never will submit.
Forever wild and free, she likes it thus;
And labours on quite happily,
Bright-eyed as the watching bird.

Barbara Liddle

DEAD FLOWERS

The flowers in the vase are dead;
Bleached petals tissue thin,
Dry and wrinkled like the skin on aged hands.
Past their prime,
They are no longer beautiful and scented,
Yet I find it hard to cast them out –
Discard without a backward glance.
I always cling to things too long;
I cannot bear to say goodbye.

Some people feel no pain at partings.
They throw the flowers of their lives away
Before they fade at all;
Put fresh blooms in their place
And never feel regret for what they've done,
For what has gone.
Shake off the past
And move into the here and now;
Life is too short to hold things fast –
You must not cling.
But what about the timing?
When and how?
Let go too soon
And much that's lovely goes to waste.
Hold on too long
And much that's lovely comes too late.
God grant me wisdom ere my life's all sped
To *know* the flowers in the vase are dead.

THE YEARS BETWEEN

It's such a long time since I squeezed
Wet sand between my toes;
Pulled petals from a daisy,
Watching them fall to earth like out-of-season snow.
I can't remember when I crouched to hold my breath
And watch a caterpillar circumnavigate a leaf.
What intervened to change it all?
What happened to the years between?

It's such a long time since I lay
On hillsides gay with gorse
To listen unafraid to plundering bees;
Or stole the rasps from off the canes
To leave on face and hands and knees
The telltale stains of juice and earth.
It's such a long time since my jealousy
Provoked me to the rape of someone's curls;
I cut them off with scissors.
I was a naughty little girl
And still recall the stormy scene that followed.
What happened to the years between?

I am no Einstein but I recognize
That time moves at a different pace from age to age
And flies just when we wish it would stand still.
I am no alchemist with magic power to alter time,
To make each hour stretch to fit whate'er I will.
And so time goes;
We cannot make the years stand still, it seems,
But yet I wonder, as the memories stir,
What happened to the years between?

LIVING WITH EPILEPSY

I fell again today but don't remember much.
My face is cut and bruised, my shoulder hurts to touch.
But no bones broken – not this time.
I'm living life as best I can, but it's not easy
Never knowing where or when
I'll fall again.
Sometimes I look into the mirror,
See a man who looks just like those other men
Who go to work and earn their pay,
Who know degrees of certainty in every waking day,
And wonder why it should be me who's cursed;
The Fates have done their very worst to me.

Don't get me wrong, I don't complain or moan;
I make a joke about a seizure in a cinema,
Collapsing in the street,
Or waking up in Casualty, alone.
The bruises on my shin,
The stitches in my chin
Are part and parcel of my life – I have no choice.
But sometimes in the night
I wish that those who pass me by
Could hear my voice – and understand.

No-one employs me – I am much too slow
And can't maintain the flow of work expected.
Catch 22 for me, you see;
If I have drugs to exercise control of fits, I'm slow;
If I have none at all, the fits increase in number, so . . . .
And then it's so embarrassing for those at work, not me;
I don't remember, so it doesn't worry me.
But other people get upset,
Don't like to see me flail about
With jerking limbs and staring eyes,
Forcing the unmentionable
To the attention of those who would deny.
They do not mean to be unkind,
They just prefer to turn their blind eye on my situation
And pretend I don't exist – a less than normal man;
While I pretend I do not care,
And hide my inner hurts as best I can.

Barbara Liddle

FOR STEVEN

I have three sons,
Tall and strong,
With sapling juices in their veins;
But more than trees, for these are men.
I have created them, tissue and bone,
Sinew and soul.
Loved and berated them,
Wept in my mother's heart
For each childhood sorrow and pain;
Weeping still for the one in three
Who yet needs me.
His is the burden,
Mine but the watcher's part.
I can do nothing for him –
There is no cure.
He learns to live with unpredictability, unsure,
Never quite knowing the where or when,
Yet knowing he will fall again.
Life isn't fair – to give me three
And then condemn the one
Who means so much to me.

*Written on St Valentine's Day 1989 after he phoned to say he'd had
another fit and ended up with three stitches in his chin, a black eye,
bruises and a cut eyelid.*

THE HONOUR OF THE GAME

Today we're playing six mixed rinks;
We start at half past two.
Try quickly saying six mixed rinks
When you've had a pint or two!
It's quite a needle match today,
Our Captain's looking grim
'Cos they're fielding County players
and they go all out to win!

Yes, it's quite a needle match today,
But at least it's our home green.
It's in beautiful condition –
The best it's ever been.
And we've had some lovely weather
So the woods are running fast;
If your weight's just that bit heavy
The damn things go rolling past!

We'd trouble making teams up;
Of new members we need more,
So we rather scraped the barrel
To make up twenty-four.
There's Stuart on Rink Four, I see,
Now there's a big surprise
For he's waiting for a cataract op.
And has trouble with his eyes!!

And little Mavis Riley
With her bias all astray
Just shakes her head and giggles
"That's the second time today!"
There's chatty Cathy Corbyn
Whose tongue's in overdrive;
Thank God she's not in my team
But playing on Rink Five.

Old Harry Bell is skipping
While I'm at number three;
He's got a very dodgy hip
And I've got a gammy knee,
But we always play together –
We know each other's game;
Good God, *their* skip is limping too –
Is he *genuinely* lame?

I'm known as Tricky Dicky
When to lucky wicks I tend,
But then their skip starts firing,
Takes the shot and wins the end!
It's a needle match alright, today,
And we're ready for our tea;
We're two down on this last end,
We need a score of three.

Reflections

I can see their skip's determined
As he straightens up his cap;
Plays his last wood on the backhand
And goes sailing through a gap.
So it all depends on Harry;
He'll have to move the jack,
'Cos the opposition's holding,
and our woods are at the back.

There's a hush around the clubhouse,
To speak would be obscene
As old Harry plays his final wood
And sends it down the green.
With a smack it hits the target,
Just as Harry meant it should
And we won the match because of it
Though no-one thought we could.

And the moral of this story,
If attention you have paid
Is "The game is never over
Till the last shot has been played."

THE BT MAN

There was a fault upon the line,
No calls were getting through.
The silence was quite nice at first
But after a day or two
I began to think all was not well
And rang the BT fault line
(from someone else's number
'cos I'd a fault on mine!)
A man came out to check my phone,
"Your problem isn't here;
your receiver's working properly,
the fault's outside, I fear.
I don't deal with outside lines," he said
"for I'm an **inside** man.
I'll tell them at the office
To send an **outside** man."
I waited in and waited in
For appearance of said man,
And two days later he arrived
In a little BT van.
He dug a hole right by my gate
And disappeared from sight.
I don't know what he did down there
But my phone still wasn't right.
He came up to the surface
And sadly shook his head;
"I'm afraid your problem's not down there,
It's up the pole instead.

But I'm a down the hole man,
I've got no head for heights.
You need an up the pole man,
He'll soon set you to rights."
And sure enough, the very next day
Another BT van
Pulled up outside my garden gate
With the promised repair man.
Well, up the pole he shimmied
In his fancy yellow hat,
While his mate stood at the bottom
And fetched him this and that.
I hope I get a rebate
For the time I had no phone,
For ten whole days without a call
Would make anybody moan.
My problem has been resolved now –
Everything's under control,
But don't send me a down the hole man
When I need one that's up the pole!

June

SIESTA

The village sits in shimmering sun,
Doing nothing, going nowhere.
It is too small – there is no road.
The bare, red rocks rise steep
Behind the single row of houses
Cloned and startling white,
Like sheets hung out to dry.

Only the sea gives access to this place;
Only the ferry comes and goes,
Chugging importantly.
Small boats rock gently at their moorings,
Doing nothing, going nowhere,
While on the hillside stunted trees
Survive against all odds,
Sending their stubborn roots
Deep into sun-bleached scree.

The village seems deserted
But behind the blind-eyed, shuttered windows
People live,
Doing nothing, going nowhere.
Stubborn as the trees above, they stay;
The ferry knows they're there
And keeps on coming.
One day, maybe, they'll tire
Of doing nothing, going nowhere,
When siesta time is done.

TIME TRAP

I hate the clock upon the wall, the watch upon my wrist;
I hate my minute-driven life, where timetables insist
That I am here at one and there at three
And somewhere else at eight.
And never dare I steal some time
In case I might be late.
Clock-ridden, clock-driven, that's my every day;
Time-ruled, time-schooled, I never get away.
When I was small and days were long
There was no time for me;
I played and slept and ate and wept
And time meant nought to me.
There was just light and dark and light again
To mark my joyous youth;
Or dry or cold or wet or cloud
Or fog or shine;
To tell the truth I heeded not the hours of each long day
For all eternity was mine.
Now when I look upon the faces of the very old
I hear them ask the time,
As old folk will.
For them the days of waiting drag slow feet
And clocks are, as bewitched, when time stands still.
They in their time warp sit and wait;
All else has gone before.
They have no future, save to wait
And wait for ever more.
Time-riding, time-biding, that's their endless day;
Time-calling, time-falling, wait and waste away.

Reflections

So, as I count the precious hours
And live my life at speed,
Forever eyeing clocks and longing to be freed
From all this daily tyranny of time,
I dream of timeless spheres
Where minutes, days and years
Mean nothing, have no place.
Where life is all tranquility,
Not this endless rushing race.
But even as I dream and hold my breath
I wonder –
Is this timelessness another name for Death?

HOUSE-HUNTING

Modern semi, central heating,
Kitchen large enough to eat in,
Three bedrooms, one en suite,
Garden, garage, quiet street.

"I wouldn't be happy here, Joe,
The lounge is far too small.
That hideous wallpaper in the hall
Would really have to go."
> "But the garden is very pretty, dear,
> There's room for a veggie patch.
> I like the dining-room hatch, dear,
> And the shops are nice and near."

Old Victorian, special features,
Former owners two Art teachers,
Off-road parking, been re-wired,
Some up-grading is required.

"I wouldn't be happy here, Joe,
It really feels damp and cold.
It's far too pricey and ever so old.
The kitchen needs gutting, you can't deny,
And all the ceilings are far too high."
> "I like the tiling, the stripped pine floors,
> Fireplaces, cornices, panelled doors.
> Plenty of scope for re-decoration;
> The challenge, my dear, is a big temptation."

Bijou apartment, river views,
25 Prince Rupert Mews,
Study/bedroom, all mod cons,
Bargain price for quick response.

"I wouldn't be happy here, Joe,
Not in this poky flat.
There's not enough room to swing a cat.
Where would all our furniture go?
I'm **not** living here, and that's final, Joe."
      "I rather like the view of the river;
        Imagine at night, with the lights all aglimmer,
        And during the day all that going and coming
        Of water-borne traffic, vibrant and humming.
        Yes, I could be happy here, make it my home;
        Yes, I could be happy here, **all on my own!**"

Barbara Liddle

POVERTY

I have dark, hungry eyes,
Lacklustre hair;
Move cautiously on shoeless feet.
Some people shun me,
Cannot bear my unwashed smell.
They'd like to think I don't exist.
My air of hopelessness stirs anger, pity, guilt or fear
But no-one really helps.
Grey is the colour of my world;
My clothes, my skin,
Their brightness stolen –
Eclipsed into forever.
I have a hunger for a better life,
And envy those who have the things I lack.

TRUTH

Where do I begin to set down thoughts
On something I can't see or feel?
And yet I know it does exist.
Some men search for it, others fear it;
Many have died for it or for the lack of it;
Irrefutable and yet ephemeral as morning mist.

It has the power to hurt or heal,
Something I neither see nor feel;
How does it survive
When those around me all contrive to stifle it?
'Thou shalt not lie' – it is a sin
But nowadays they call it 'spin'
And seem to think it no bad thing.
Where does it live – in heart or mind?
Oh, why is the TRUTH so hard to find?

Barbara Liddle

WILDFIRE (Arizona/Colorado, June 2002)

I heard the screaming first,
The death throes of my kin,
Long before the smoke came
Or the hot, dry air that chokes.

The animals are running,
Running for their lives
Before the fire-bite crackle of devouring flames,
But we cannot run.

Our roots bind us to the earth that nurtured us;
We cannot of our own free will let go.
And so we stand to face our Armageddon.
Spruce and fir, aspen and pine.
Man's puny efforts are in vain;
There is not rain enough
To quench destruction such as this,
Put out the fires of Hell.

A TIME AND PLACE

A time and place; a place in time-
All to be captured in a rhyme.
So many times, so many places
Buildings, colours, sounds and faces.

Pérouges, small city mediaeval;
Narrow, cobbled streets and high stone arches
Where echoes from the past still seemed to float on scented
    breezes.
A simple church with wide, worn steps and whitewashed walls;
Two round-eyed windows spilling rainbows on the floor.
Half-timbered houses sleeping in the sun
Behind their dark brown shutters,
Brightened by window-boxes gay with scarlet flowers;
And in a tiny, secret courtyard
Glimpsed only from a neighbouring roof,
Three knot gardens, gloriously green,
With plants for cooking, plants for healing,
And, being French, a third devoted to l'amour.

If in the past these empty streets and silent walls
Had known the clash of steel, the sounds of strife
They were not there that day;
Only the sense of times gone by;
A place of beauteous age and mystery.

July

CRETE

I remember Crete.
Scent of bougainvillea, charcoal grilling, coconut oil;
The taste of salt sweat on my lips,
The burning sand beneath bare feet.
Tides of gaudy colour, as the tourists ebb and flow,
While bodies brown, inert, lie on the beach
Like some strange flotsam.
Sound of a thousand crickets' songs
Borne on a perfumed breeze
Above the dusty olive trees.
All this, encapsulated in the heat –
My memory of Crete

Barbara Liddle

THE SWIMMING POOL
(Le Tivoli Hotel, Agadir, Morocco)

Around the pool the bodies lie,
From palest white to deepest brown,
And all shades in between.
Some patchy, some a smooth all-over tan
With not a strap mark to be seen.
I envy all that smooth perfection
But tell myself, upon reflection,
We cannot **all** be lilies of the field
Who toil not, neither do they spin,
While cultivating such a flawless skin.
Some people swim determinedly, like me,
Cleaving the turquoise water
Like some paint-box seal.
Young men show off by diving in,
Others eschew such healthy exercise
And lie inert upon their chosen bed,
Feeling the heat sink deep into their bones,
Limbs carefully anointed with sweet-smelling oil
As though they would be living sacrifices to the sun.
Perhaps we should be gently basting them
And wrapping them in Bacofoil!
Young girls in miniscule bikinis
Flaunt figures which have not yet housed a child,
While bolder ones go topless,
Sporting breasts as small and firm as unripe fruit,

Reflections

And old men who have seen it all before
Sip ice-cold beers and slumber fitfully
Beneath the striped umbrellas,
Dreaming of days gone by.
Sweet lethargy of indolence;
I know it will not last for ever
But thank the gods for this small pleasure
And this time of self-indulgence.

THE NATCHEZ TRACE, U.S.A.

The birds from tall trees fling the self-same song
That someone heard a hundred years ago,
Along the Natchez Trace.
No-one fears today strange shadows in the woods;
Imagines death or treachery in unknown face.
A hundred simmering summers
And a hundred chilling snows
Have faded in time's memory till no-one knows
Exactly what was done or said.
And yet the voices of the dead tell tales of long ago
And echo loud and long 'cross time and space
To let the traveller of today know
Here was history made, along the Natchez Trace.

*During a coach tour of America's Deep South we followed
part of the trail which used to bring the fur-trappers from up
north through hostile Indian country down to New Orleans
to sell their winter's haul of furs. This was called the Natchez
Trace and, as the coach rolled on, I wrote this poem at the
back of my diary.*

AFTER PUGLIA – What is a House?

A chamber tomb was once my home.
My fires destroyed the earlier frescoes on the walls
But left the proof of my existence on the stones.
Such simple things we leave behind;
Fragments of pots, intricate patterns of mosaic,
Though nothing remains of us, not even bones.

No, nothing remains of us, not even bones;
Though we leave clues behind for those with eyes to see;
Piecing together the fragments of our lives,
Telling the where and when and why of who we were,
And how our race survived, or how we died.

And shall our race today survive, or shall we die
Like those before?
Leaving mute traces of graffiti on the walls.
Two thousand years from now will someone excavate the ruins of
    the Dome?
And speculate upon its purpose.
Who put it there, and why?
Or was it once perhaps somebody's home?

Barbara Liddle

MALTA

High on a terrace perched above a bay,
Old people sit dreaming
While wintry sunshine seeps gently into tired bones.
Crumbling arches of yellow stone
Make windows of the distant view
While present, past and future fuse
Into the mellowness of time stood still.
Pigeons scatter and re-form
Before the onslaught of a toddler's feet,
And still the tired old faces turn towards the warmth,
Like human sunflowers,
As shadows slowly lengthen.
I see the domes of distant churches
On the skyline to my right,
And to my left the patient sea beyond the harbour walls
Stretches unbroken to a cloudless sky.
Down through the centuries these battlements and bastions
Have kept invaders out,
Withstanding cannon balls and shells and bombs,
Until today the echoes only softly ring
With children's laughter
And the flutter of a startled pigeon's wings.

Reflections

Long years ago did anxious watchers on the walls
Believe that peace would ever come
To bless this spot with sweet serenity?
Or did they die, defending what was theirs?
Never to know those self-same walls that cost them dear
Would stand long after they were gone,
To be a restful garden for a traveller, such as me.

Poem written on the back of a paper bag while sitting in the Upper Barrakka Gardens in Valletta on a Sunday afternoon in November 1988.

Barbara Liddle

TUSCAN HOLIDAY

Piazzas and Palazzos,
I have seen them by the score,
And martyr'd Saints and frescoes
Behind each Cathedral door.
I have gazed at gilded ceilings,
Trodden ancient, cobbled ways;
Two thousand years of history
In only seven days!
And what will I remember?
What memories remain?
It isn't names and dates, my friend,
My inner eye retains.

Balconies geranium-splash'd,
Stone Portas wide and high;
Sharp-pointed cypresses about to write
Upon the canvas of the sky.
Clustered tapestries of roof tiles,
Washing drying on a line;
The smell of fresh-baked pizza,
The taste of sweet red wine.
The play of light and shadow
In narrow alleyways;
Welcome coolness of the evenings
After hot and dusty days.
My photographs are there for you
To see where I have been,
But never will they capture
What my inner eye has seen.

CALVI IN CORSICA

Sometimes heartache becomes a permanent part of life;
Sadness almost tangible,
Like layers of soft grey velvet.
Odd, how you long to be free,
Even as you fold the layers close around you.
Sadness becomes comforting
When you can't imagine anything else.

But here I feel the sadness slowly lifting out of me,
Like wet pavements steaming in the sun
After sudden summer rain.
Not now, today, or even soon
But one day, some day
I shall again be whole;
Feel the warmth reaching the frozen corners of my soul.

High above the town there stands the Citadel
While narrow streets below are bright
With towels and T-shirts for the beach;
Flip-flops and postcards, gaudy souvenirs.
Down by the harbour sun-sated tourists take their ease
At café tables shaded by umbrellas, blue and green and red;
Grateful for the benison of sea-cooled breeze.
You would have loved it here, but you are dead,
And I am here alone.

Barbara Liddle

TUNISIA

The soldier olive trees stand to attention on the plain;
Impenetrable lines of prickly pears
Are interspersed with graceful eucalyptus.
The land is winter-lush, water-rich and green
Though houses mostly look unkempt,
Their crumbling walls and blistered paint a quiet reproach.
Washing hangs limp upon a windless roof,
As hungry cats weave in and out of shadows.
Old men crouch motionless in one small patch of sun
And rest their calloused hands on tired knees.
Five times a day the faithful kneel to pray;
Faith binds together all the fragile pieces of their lives.
Believers know, when all else fails,
That faith remains.

VACANCES À MONTAGNY

Une église ancienne, les ombres des traboules,
Les pierres sous mes pieds, ce sont mes souvenirs.
Un bouchon Lyonnais, une fontaine dans le parc,
La musique de poêmes, tout ça me fait plaisir.

Les fleuves et les collines, l'air frais sur mon visage,
La verdure de jeunes vignes, ce sont mes souvenirs.
Le doux parfum d'été, le gout de vin nouveau,
L'amitié et l'amour, tout ça me fait plaisir.

Ferrat et Aragon, j'aime beaucoup leurs chansons;
La tristesse et la joie, ce sont mes souvenirs.
Les sourires des enfants, les charmes de mes amis,
La mémoire d'une prière, tout ça me fait plaisir.

*I was staying with friends Guy and Pierrette in
Montagny, near Lyon, when I was tempted to write
this poem in French – may the reader please forgive
any errors of construction!*

August

MARTHA'S KITCHEN

My kitchen was always white and clean and lifeless;
Hers was not.
On the table the remnants of breakfast –
A ravaged grapefruit, toast-crumbed plate
And half a cup of coffee.
The morning's post, roughly opened then abandoned,
And yesterday's paper, crossword unfinished;
The fridge door covered in twee little magnets
And smudgy crayoned pictures.
Assorted pot plants on the window sill,
Struggling to survive assiduous watering;
Apples, greenly golden, in a wooden bowl
And well-thumbed cookery books;
She had a light touch with pastry, I recall.
A pair of much-used secateurs
On the floor beside her gardening shoes,
And everywhere a sense of busy-ness and urgency,
Of being loved, and loving.

HOUSES

Sometimes I envy the people who stay;
Contented and settled, never moving away,
But then I remember the houses I've known –
The red brick, the granite, the stucco, the stone.
So many partings, and so many moves;
So many times to put down new roots.
So many houses to turn into homes.
Terraced or semi-detached or alone;
The red brick, the granite, the stucco, the stone.
An end of terrace, grey stone house
Confronting Scottish gales and snow;
The place where I was young.
It seemed so spacious then, so tall;
But later, when with adult eyes I looked again,
I thought it small.
The house beside the river I remember well,
In grey and grimy Glasgow, with its dirty, city smell.
Pulsing dockyards, screeching tramcars,
Stockpiled tea and sugar in the cellar
While the bombs rained down on Clydeside.
Solid and squat, in slabs of stone,
The house that I was married from;
And then a neat, small bungalow
With neat, small windows and a matching plot
Wherein the neat, small concrete shelter brooded;
Relic of a war that would not be forgot.
South then to rural England, and a rented house;

Reflections

Cold and unwelcoming,
Acres of brown, unfurrowed floors to clean,
While in the outhouse lived the smell of sleeping apples.
Thatched cottage down a country lane,
Holly and honeysuckle, drowsy summer days;
Fields of corn and birdsong dawnings;
Crooked boards beneath my feet
And memories, like lavender, forever sweet.
Old town house, three storeys tall;
Sash windows rattling in the winter winds,
And honey-coloured panelling in living-room and hall.
New town semi- in a row of breeze-block clones;
No character can flesh and form on such bare bones.
So many partings and so many moves,
So many times to put down new roots.
So many houses to turn into homes.
Terraced and semi-detached or alone,
The red brick, the granite, the stucco, the stone.

Barbara Liddle

SHADOWS

We are but shadows on the page of Life;
We have no substance, shape or form.
Deep in the hearts of men we dwell,
Unseen, unvoiced, undying, yet unborn.

Why did we never have the chance to grow?
To show the world what we could be?
Was there not time enough or opportunity?
Did someone's courage fail
When it was time to set us free?

Unfulfilled dreams –
We have no substance, shape or form;
Sad shadows on the page of Life,
Not quite forgotten, but forlorn.

EARTH

I am the planet, mankind calls Earth;
I am the Earth being ravaged by Man.
I am the forest, gradually dwindling;
I am the creature facing extinction;
I am the air, full of pollution,
I am the icecap, rapidly melting.

I am the logger, felling the forests;
I am the hunter, stalking the creatures.
I'm the creator of greenhouse gases
Making a hole in the ozone layer.
I am the seeds of my own destruction,
Killing the planet, mankind calls Earth.

Barbara Liddle

LOVE LIFE OF A TEMP

It was half past two on a Tuesday afternoon
When I first fell in love with Ben.
He was almost unaware of me standing there
As he made little doodles with his pen.

I was 'temping' at the time, I was slightly past my prime,
But I'd worked in lots of offices before.
My work was accurate and neat, the secretarial elite
Had long ago enrolled me in its corps.

So at half past two on a Tuesday afternoon
It was not with expectations of romance
That I knocked upon the door of his room on the fifth floor
With my shorthand notebook clutched in well-trained hands.

His dictation voice was confident and pleasant to the ear;
He hardly ever changed a word, his punctuation clear.
He didn't pace about the room, he sat calm and quite relaxed,
He even smiled from time to time as he asked me to read back
What he had said – and he nodded as I read.

We worked very well together, but he never thought of love
As I typed reports and documents for him to sign;
As I typed his letters and his memos, with my heart in every line.
I was just Miss Jones, the agency temp,
Miss Jones from the typing pool.
I was just Miss Jones, secretarial help –
Silly romantic fool.

But temping jobs are short and sharp, and temps just never stay;
I worked for Ben for three whole weeks, and then I went away.
I never said that I was leaving – he didn't seem to care
That I'd typed and dreamed, and worked and schemed;
He was sublimely unaware.

So I went away with my broken heart and I temped for somebody
    new;
And the very next week, at a quarter to three,
I first fell in love with Hugh.

Barbara Liddle

THE COLOUR OF HOPE

If black is the colour of despair, what is the colour of hope?
Is it blue, like a clear summer sky
Or the blue of an innocent baby's eye?
Is it green, like the mist of new leaves in Spring
Or the green of an emerald in somebody's ring?
Is it yellow, or purple, or orange, or pink?
Does it have to be coloured at all do you think?
Is it clear, is it shiny, does it sparkle and glow?
Does it have a special shape? Or a smell, do you know?
When hope comes, will I feel it?
Will I know that it's there?
For I've certainly known the touch of despair,
And I've sighed and I've cried and I've struggled to cope.
Won't someone please tell me the colour of hope?

THE METAMORPHOSIS OF EMILY

She always moved quickly,
Flitting from toy to toy,
Attracted by the colours.

Her arms changed first,
Stopped clinging round my neck.
Limpet hands welded to her tiny waist,
The space within becoming delicately shaded,
Lightly fluttering.

In sleep she curled up like a frond of fern,
And in the morning legs had fused together
Into a body soft and faintly furry.
Her lovely face had shrunk to something black and alien
But still, in wholeness, such a thing of beauty.

I touched her gently and the two wings stirred,
Quivered into flight - and she was gone;
Off into the garden, revelling in the sunshine,
Flitting from flower to flower.

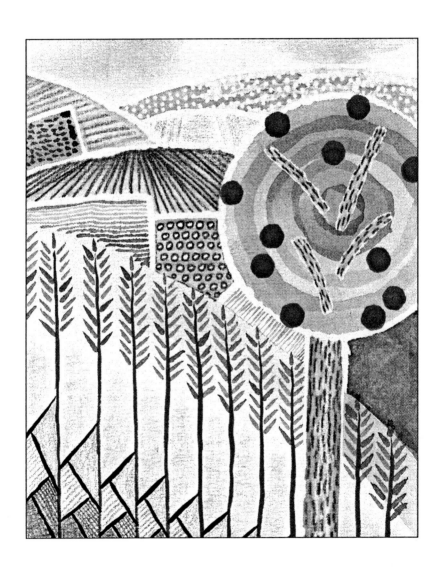

September

DREAMS OF DRAGONS

Dreams of dragons, mystic monsters,
Pressing with their scaly feet upon the clouds
And bringing rain.
Deep, deep within us all lie dragons
Which our consciousness subdues.
Yet, though we fear, we cannot quite destroy
The dragons in our being,
With awesome power for good or evil;
For they are part of us and must remain.
The Freudian Id
With horns and scales and breathing fire.
And though we praise St George
And others of his ilk for slaying such
We yet, if truthful to ourselves,
Admire the dragons deep within,
And will not yield them up
To alien touch.

Composed in 1989 after reading 'Dreams of Dragons' by Lyall Watson

ST ANDREW'S CHURCH

At the corner of a street I saw a single spire
Pointing accusingly towards a clear blue sky.
The church itself was gone –
A victim of alleged development;
Only the solitary spire was left to mark the place,
To tell the passer-by,
That people once had worshipped there
With voices raised in anthem
And heartbeats hushed in prayer.
Wavering faith, buttressed by ritual,
As were the outer walls by stone;
And only the blackened spire left,
Witnessing alone.
Gone were the story'd windows
With their stained glass Saints and Seraphs
Captured in coloured fragments
Like a rainbow's tears.
Gone was the pulpit and the altar too,
And in their place there stood a giant crane,
Grotesquely angular and metal yellow.
Herald of change and the ubiquitous building site.
But even as I gazed
And pondered on a church's loss,
The transverse of the crane in silhouette
Behind the spire became a cross.

Reflections

So, for a moment, both were joined,
The church spire and the crane,
To show to those with eyes to see
The symbol of Christ's passion and his pain.

*Written on the demise of St Andrew's Church,
Finch Road, Douglas, Isle of Man*

Barbara Liddle

FRUSTRATED MUSE

I wonder if the poets of renown sat down
And gazed, like me, upon a pristine page
And cursed the fickle Muse
That had deserted them awhile.
Did Wordsworth frown and bite his nails
Or worse
Until he wandered lonely as a cloud
O'er Lakeland hills
And, thus inspired, immortalized the daffodils?
I can't imagine Browning stuck for words
Or Tennyson a rhyme;
Their artistry is manifest in every single line
They ever wrote.
But were they sometimes, unbeknown to me,
Quite at a loss?
Did T. S. Eliot toss off verses with a golden pen?
Or did he try and try and try again
Before composing something like The Hollow Men?
How many times did Keats rewrite his poems
Until satisfied?
Or Shakespeare sigh o'er couplets that defied
His nimble skill?
Perhaps they too despaired
And cast aside an ode half-formed;
Aborted brainchild, like some foetus not yet grown,
Until they could produce a masterpiece
That they'd be proud to own.
So shall I choose to think,
For thus it comforts me.
That I am one of such illustrious company.

FRUSTRATED MUSE (2)

I feel a poem coming on;
The words are chasing round and round.
There is no pattern, shape or form,
The idea still unborn;
And yet I feel a poem coming on.
My mental tissues are possessed,
My brain obsessed.
Compulsively my pen must write
And fill the blankness of the page
While inwardly I rage
That nothing beautiful or bold is yielded up,
Only the ordinary, cliché trite.
Poetic fancy thrown upon the wheel
Does not emerge a thing of beauty,
Merely shapeless clay;
So I must wait,
Create my masterpiece
Another time, another day.

Barbara Liddle

TIDES

The man is slowly dying;
He knows it, but says nothing.
It will not happen today, or even tomorrow,
But one day soon . . . .
The woman shares his dragging days,
The broken pattern of his nights.
Unspoken questions swirl and eddy in her mind,
But are not voiced.
How can she ask, are you in pain?
What can I do?
Are you afraid?

She touches him often, lovingly,
Transfusing her warmth, her strength,
But says nothing.
Each day the unseen enemy within
Takes stronger hold.
Each day, they know, brings death a little closer,
Yet neither speaks of it.
Words will not make it go away.

The silence hangs between them,
Heavy, impenetrable,
Denying stark reality.
The tide is rising,
Slow, inexorable,
And when it ebbs there will be nothing left.
Only an aching memory of what once was.

Reflections

Far out, on mudflats of the Solway Firth,
The witches used to drown.
Tied to stout posts embedded in the sand,
Helpless they'd stand, watching the killer tide
Creep ever closer, till they died.
But that was long ago.
Today the posts and witches are not there,
Though tides, relentless, rise and fall.
And those caught in life's tide
May still be drowned.

Barbara Liddle

NEIGHBOURS

I envy you the even tenour of your life;
Your undisturbed and quiet hours.
Your house is always tidy, and your mind the same;
You never have to rush from place to place with claims
Upon your time, your energy, your brain.
You live forever in the storm's calm eye;
Protected, shielded and unruffled
Whilst trials and tribulations pass you by.
I envy you.

You envy me?
How strange that your perception so misleads,
When all the time my needs, unanswered and unvoiced,
Leave me no choice but yearning idleness.
Demands upon my time are few
Because I am not loved like you.
Nobody turns to me for help, advice;
Draws on my strength, my cheerfulness,
Or feels twice-blessed for having turned to me.
Enclosed, enfolded by your muddles and your chores,
The better life by far is yours.
I envy you.

AGONY AUNTS

We had a small Convention, in Weston-super-mare;
Forty-seven Agony Aunts all gathered there.
There was Clarice from the Clarion, and Mavis from the Mail,
And somebody called Julian, who writes his stuff in Braille!
There was Lucy from a teenage mag. that has a 'Lovelorn' page
And a very flamboyant woman who used to be on the stage.
We all compared the postbags that daily we receive
And wondered in our heart of hearts if we really could believe
The letters people send us about the problems in their lives;
Irritating neighbours, interfering parents, alcoholic husbands,
    unfaithful wives,
Teenage angst and worries about sex and spots and such,
And everybody's questions about love – too little or too much.
Isn't anybody happy? Do they have to make a fuss?
Is the world so full of problems that they need to write to us?
We shouldn't be complaining; we should be overjoyed;
It's because of all their problems that we are all employed;
But we're none of us very qualified, not trained psychologists;
Glibly handing out answers, like expert therapists.
We hope we're giving comfort, wrapped up in our advice,
But we never discover the outcome – they never write to us twice.
It's a funny old life being an Agony Aunt, sorting out other folks'
    woes,
Selecting which problems to deal with, and what to reject, I
    suppose.
I really enjoyed the Convention in Weston-super-mare,
And if they hold another one perhaps I'll meet you there.
It's good to know there are others, doing the same thing I do,
Some of us better than others, most of us honest and true.
Perhaps you've read my column, perhaps you don't give a damn,
But my name is confidential, so you'll never know who I am.

October

DESERTED COTTAGE
(on seeing the ruins on a hillside in the Isle of Man)

Once you were someone's home
With hearthstone warm and welcome bright.
Your sheltering walls gave comfort on a stormy night
And peat smoke gently curled above the chimney there.
Now crumbling stones lie mute
And weeds take root
Where once the fire did burn;
Your sightless windows look in vain
For man's return
And rotting rafters mourn
The fallen roof and lintel bare.

Barbara Liddle

STILLBORN

Every poet has his own collection;
Lines that never made it to a poem.
Lines that capture the imagination
Sometimes never grow beyond their first conception.

"Every father casts a shadow"
That was one to conjure with.
Hours I spent with visions in my head
Of my father, long since dead.
But, somehow, rhyme and rhythm wouldn't follow;
What I wrote was dull and lifeless,
Empty scribbles on a page
And a single, haunting line.

A line can set you on an untrod path,
Leading onwards, who knows where.
Round and round in endless circles,
Never ever getting there.

These are my stillborn children;
These lines that never grew into a rounded whole.
Born of my poetic fancy, part of my poetic soul,
I cannot yet abandon, bury them;
For some day, when the muse is kind,
I will release them from suspended animation,
Breathe new life into their bare and brittle bones;
Waking them to new creation.

THE BUCHAN BALL

I felt like Cinderella at the Ball;
I hardly knew a soul at all
Except the three friends who'd invited me.
Ladies all, without a man,
Feeling like an also-ran
In that black bow-tied company.
The early part was not a strain;
I stood about and sipped champagne
While those who knew the in-crowd
Moved about from group to group.
I smiled and chatted, quite polite,
And thought uneasily about the night
As more and more the in-crowd milled about,
Just like excited chickens in a coop.
The fashions all around me
Were a wondrous sight to see;
Velvet, satin, beaded, bare,
Perfumed bodies, lacquered hair.
At least my dress was just as elegant as theirs
Although I had no man with me.
Eventually we moved through to the dining-room,
To take our places there.
Slow moving river of dinner jacket black and colours fair.
Our little party swelled to six
By two more ladies on their own
And so we sat amid a hundred pairs,
Six ladies all alone.

Barbara Liddle

The meal was quite delicious
But then I needn't dwell
On melon and beef Wellington;
You know the format well.
But on each table at each place
There lay a blue and silver card,
Beglittered and beribboned,
And this is where the evening became hard.
For on each lady's card
The gentlemen inscribed their name
Against the dance they wished to claim;
And wives and girlfriends smugly smiled
To see their cards completed, hearts beguiled.
Or else a beauty, never in her life bereft,
Flirted outrageously
And said she'd only one dance left.
I kept my social smile pinned firmly on my face;
The losers aren't supposed to sulk
When others win the race.
But, oh, it hurts when others dance
And melt into the beat
While you sit frozen, all alone,
And hide your tapping feet.

Reflections

Six ageing wallflowers at a dance,
No partners then, or ever – no romance,
Just grim determination to pretend,
To hold your fragile poise
When all the time you want to run away –
Escape the noise,
The sight of other couples having a good time
While inwardly you grieve
And check your watch with anxious eyes
To see if you can leave
Before the game becomes impossible to play – too hard;
Before the façade crumbles and the teardrops fall
Upon an empty card.
Like Cinderella, I too fled at midnight
And shed a tear or two,
But only in the quietness of my lonely room
For my memories of you.

Barbara Liddle

WEDDING DAY

I sing in the Parish Church choir,
We practise each week, Friday night,
And when we're robed up in our 'blue'
We're quite an attractive sight.

With an average age of 64
We sing mostly in tune – when we can;
The balance of voices is not very good
With 15 sopranos, 4 altos, 1 man!

Apart from Sunday services
We sing at funerals too
And often for a wedding –
Which is much more fun to do.

We have the best view of the bride
And the guests assembled there.
We are critical of fashions – and hats –
And what Mothers and Bridesmaids wear.

The men are not interesting – soberly dressed,
In morning suit, pinstripe or kilt.
Nine times out of ten they don't even speak up
When making their vow that they will't.

The brides are all lovely, I have to admit,
I ain't seen a plain one yet,
But the dresses they wear leave a lot of flesh bare –
I wonder if Vicar's upset!

Reflections

And as for the trains that most of them have,
To me it's a terrible shame
For a dress that cost pounds to be trailed on the ground;
It'll never be quite the same.

The bridesmaids are usually pretty in pink,
Or cream, or lilac, or blue,
With flowers in their hair and a tiny bouquet,
Matching shoes that are painfully new.

And as for the Mothers – well, they mustn't clash;
I bet they've conferred long before.
Well, you couldn't have two in the very same hue,
Wishing t'other would sink through the floor.

In my day the guests all wore hats
And behaved with proper decorum,
But these days it seems as if anything goes –
Mini skirts and see-through tops – we oldies just deplore 'em.

There's always the wedding video
With a camera recording it all,
Not just the posed photographs taken outside
But inside the church candid shots wall to wall.

And at nearly all the weddings
Bride and groom look oh so young,
Rushing into married life
Before youthful flings have been flung.

I hope they'll both be happy
For all the years ahead.
They confidently make their vows,
The age-old words are said.

Triumphal Wedding March resounds
As down the aisle they go,
And all of us remember
Our own day, long ago.

Then family and guests file out
To the sound of wedding chimes,
And everyone is smiling,
For it's such a happy time.

And back inside the Vestry
We put our robes away
Until we have to sing again
At another Wedding Day.

THE AMATEUR PHOTOGRAPHER

The camera sits, inanimate, upon a tripod shiny-legged.
The man behind the lens is like a little boy
Playing at Christmas with an unfamiliar toy.
Others look on, quietly amused,
As he adjusts the height of legs recalcitrant
That stand uncertainly on marble floor,
(And seem determined not to get it right!)

Distance, focus, light and shutter speed
Are matters all of great concern;
Minute adjustments needed for the perfect shot.
A great photographer he most certainly is not!
But tolerant affection holds his models in their pose;
A little waiting is not much to ask
For one we love – and, who knows?
When other memories grow dim
The photograph will still be there
And those who love will smile
And still remember him.

SUNSET

The fury of the storm abating,
Here's a sky with glorious colours flaming.
A stippled firmament brazen with power;
Armageddon fires amid the violet clouds,
Like molten lava 'cross the skyline.
Here is the death of day in fiercest exultation,
Screaming defiance at the night,
Refusing to yield the heavens to softer shades of silver.
More intense, a narrower band,
The gleam where earth meets sky;
The highest canopy already dark in muted indigo;
A catafalque of black the distant hills,
With resting clouds a purple coronet above.
Yet still the sky glows crimson,
Fierceness fading even as I gaze,
Amazed that so much beauty should be there for but a moment.
The pulse of dying day grows weaker;
Only the faintest glimmer now remains.
I mourn its passing,
Even as I know there will be other sunsets, other skies;
But none like this.
This is a gift that none can keep.

November

RUTH

You look at me with eyes so wide and clear;
No jealousy, no hatred, cynicism, fear.
You have not learned yet to distrust
The people that you meet.
Not yet destroyed,
The faith you have in all mankind,
And to the darker side of human nature
You are blind.

You speak to me with candour, not with guile;
Your little face so serious, yet when you smile
You brighten everything around, and all the while
You labour to absorb and understand
My answers to your ceaseless questionings.
You touch me with a hand that's smooth,
And warm, and small;
Pulsing with boundless energy.
You are enthralled by Life's excitements.
Afraid to miss one moment of its mysteries and charms,
Unwillingly you go to bed,
Though sleep is lurking there behind your eyes.
You dream, untroubled, undisturbed,
And greet each morning with a glad surprise.

In you I see my own eternity,
Ephemeral glimpses of times past and times to come.
I wish I could encapsulate your youth,
Keeping forever perfect
All that you do and say and are;
Fast-freeze the flavour of your joy and truth,
Essential essence of my grandchild, Ruth.

Barbara Liddle

THE GREY ONES

There is a stranger
In the chair beside the window;
The chair where Edith used to sit,
Dwarfed by the amaryllis in the plastic pot.
She looks like all the others,
Sad and shrivelled,
With bandages on stick-like legs.
The nurses call her Doris,
But she does not speak.
Why should one make a noise
When there is nothing left to say?
Who listens anyway?

Nobody tells you "Edith died".
They draw the curtains and pretend,
And when the curtains are pulled back
There is no trace.
Erased, as though she'd never been;
The bed made up with sheets and pillows,
Crisp and clean.
The locker bare, no cards, no flowers,
No slippers by the bed.
But no-one ever tells you "Edith's dead".
Only a stranger in the chair
Beside the window where she sat,
Beside the amaryllis in the plastic pot.

Reflections

We did not mean to grow so old,
So helpless and so frail.
We have been useful in our time, our prime.
We were not always as you see us now –
Grey people – hair, skin, lives, all grey.
We have no more to give,
And find it hard to tell the days apart,
But still that traitor heart keeps beating,
Making us live a little longer
Than we wish or care;
Until the time another stranger takes our place
And sits beside the window in our chair.

COMPUTER BLUES

My computer's on the blink and I feel that I could scream;
Every time I push the buttons
'CABLE DISCONNECTED' comes up upon my screen.
I think it was the lightning that upset it 'cos I woke up in the
    night
And downstairs in my study there was a strange blue light.
My computer in the corner had a message on the screen,
'CABLE DISCONNECTED' in blue letters;
Whatever could it mean?
The thunder kept on thundering and the lightning lit the sky;
I didn't know how to fix it – well, I didn't even try.
I switched off at the socket and went back upstairs to bed;
"I'll sort it in the morning" to myself I firmly said.
Now, at this point in the proceedings,
I think I should explain
That I'm a technophobe par excellence;
From handling things mechanical I totally abstain.
My car's an automatic, I just turn the ignition key;
The microwave and washing machine are mysteries to me.
And likewise with the Hoover and the Flymo for outside;
I just turn them on and turn them off –
Don't know what goes on inside.
But my computer has been programmed to drive me up the
    wall,
And my row of fancy manuals never seem to help at all.
On-line banking and insurance, on-line booking for a flight,
On-line shopping for my groceries, on-line gambling day and
    night;

Reflections

On-line this and on-line that for almost everything we do,
When I much prefer the human touch, with real people –
Well, don't you?
So I haven't fixed my computer – it's still blank as blank can be,
And I'm doing everything by hand, which really pleases me.
I am **talking** to my friends and I'm **writing** to them too,
'Cos I can't send them an e-mail while I've got computer blues.

Barbara Liddle

CHANGE OF ADDRESS

Like a proud lady stripped,
Naked and ashamed,
My house stands empty and forlorn.
I, who loved it so, have done this thing;
Left empty hooks upon the walls
Where once my pictures hung,
And packed in cardboard boxes
All the ornaments and bric-a-brac of life
Alongside memories of happy times gone by.

Do I imagine that the walls rebuke me for my fickleness?
The empty hearth reproaches me for leaving it behind?
Do windows, now unframed by pretty curtains, feel abandoned?
I do not mean to be unkind.

As mournful as the foghorn's lonely note,
My spirits droop as low as roses after rain.
My footsteps echo in the empty rooms,
And in my heart there is an ache, the pain
Of parting from this special place, my home.

A PILL FOR ALL SEASONS

Pills in a bottle, small and round,
With childproof cap and printed label;
Two to be taken three times a day,
Convenience capsules to keep pain away.

Pills in a flat sheet, sealed in foil;
Keep to the dosage, don't forget,
One to be taken, just one each day
Clinically keeping conception at bay.

Pills in containers, kept by the bed,
Easing my sleeplessness, dispelling dread;
Valium, Librium, Mogadon – these
Bring comfort and respite with consummate ease.

And when I travel, my stomach feels queasy,
No need to worry – the remedy's easy.
Pills to combat excess fat,
Pills for this, and pills for that,
Pills to fight a mild infection,
Pills to cure my indigestion.
A shelf full of tablets to cure any ill;
Peace of mind, disguised as a pill.

When I die and patiently wait
With others by the Pearly Gate, will I be given a harp to play?
What will the kindly St Peter say?
Will he tell me to go away?
Or hand me a bottle of Vitamin A,
One to be taken, three times a day!

Barbara Liddle

DON'T MAKE ME PROMISES

Don't make me promises;
Not if you don't mean the honeyed words
That drip so sweetly from your practised tongue.
Don't speak me words of love;
That you have uttered many times before
When you and I were young.
Don't touch my hand
With lingering fingertip,
Arousing passions long ago subdued,
When I surrendered to your deep embrace.
Don't look at me
With dark and dangerous eyes
That bring remembrance in their depths
And not forgetfulness of voice and form and face.
Don't come into my life *now,*
Awakening everything I knew;
When I have tried so hard, my love,
To bury every memory of you.

December

THE CHRISTMAS LIST

Dear Santa,

Do you ignore the voice of those no longer young?
Or do you care about the grown-up children too?
It is a long time since I wrote to you.
Somehow the years between have gone – I don't know where,
But now that I've some time to spare,
I thought I'd let you know about my Christmas List.
As usual, I've missed the time for posting but then it takes me
  longer now
To do all sorts of things that in my youth could be accomplished
  in a flash.

It must be nice to stay the same, the way you do,
And never feel the weight of years that slow us down
And limit life with every passing day.
High on my list please, Santa, is a little bit of oil
For these old joints of mine;
To help me be more sprightly as I move about.
New eyes, that I may view the world with realism, yet with joy;
Without a doubt, rose-tinted spectacles are just a ploy
To cover up the sadness of reality.
New eyes are better, far, to see things as they really are,
And then we all can try to make the world a better place,
To start each day with peaceful heart and smiling face.
Crystallised sunshine in a flowery pot;
For days when skies are grey and not so hot;
When I believe that all around me have forgotten I'm still here.

It isn't much to ask for, Santa dear.
I'm very lucky really, for I have a lot of friends and memories
And souvenirs from days of long ago;
So my Christmas List is very small, but I wanted you to know –
For I feel it very strongly, and I know that it is true –
There are old, old children, Santa, who still believe in you.

This poem was written for my Mother, who kept it sellotaped to the locker beside her hospital bed until she died at the age of 91.

AFTERMATH

I'm suffering from P.C.T.*
A parlous state I'm in.
Got an overloaded stomach and an over-flowing bin,
Full of screwed up Christmas paper,
Empty bottles, cans of Coke.
Christmas Day was really wicked!
But the aftermath's no joke!!
My Christmas tree's still twinkling with its baubles, balls and
    lights;
But there's nothing very festive about the way I feel tonight.
There's only so much Disney I can watch upon T.V.
And another sodding mince pie will be the death of me!

I've sung my Christmas carols, and I've spread my Christmas
    cheer,
But I'd really rather hibernate when we reach this time of year.
I've posted Christmas parcels, Christmas cards sent by the score,
But I've lost my Christmas spirit and I can't take any more.
I've pulled my Christmas crackers and I've worn my silly hats;
I've decked the hall with holly and put Welcome on the mat.
I have given to the postman and the milkman and the rest;
I've even pinned some mistletoe upon my scrawny chest.
But I'd really rather hibernate in a secret, silent place,
Far away from Father Christmas and the rest of the human race.
This disenchanted person, please believe me, you hardly ever see,
But I'm sick to death of Christmas and I'm suffering from P.C.T.

* Post Christma Trauma

RESURRECTION

Here be bugs an' snails an' blight
Here be the colours of delight
Here be spiders, greenfly, weeds
Here be rainbow promises in seeds

Here be earth that's rich and dark
Here be stones'd break your back
Here be worms and crawlin' things
Here be bluebells in the Spring

Here be grass an' here be trees
Here be plantin' on your knees
Here be prunin' – seems insane
To cut 'un down for to grow again

I been a gardener all my life
Loved my garden, dear as a wife
Seen God's message everywhere
In a garden, bloomin' fair
Watched things die and watched 'em grow
Resurrection's true, I know

BIRDS IN WINTER

The snowflakes twirl and twist and tease;
On roofs and walls and roads the blanket clings,
And in deserted playgrounds sits on all the swings.
A cold, pure magic only the eye of childhood sees.

Birds cluster together in the trees,
Bare branches blossoming with fluttering wings;
Here in this white and silent world, where no bird sings,
The snow soon swallows up my meagre scraps of bread and
    cheese.

I am too old to see the magic any more,
I am afraid, in winter's grip,
To venture out beyond my door.

But birds, untethered to the earth, fear not to slip;
High in the leaden sky they soar,
Defiant in the face of snowfall's icy nip.

Barbara Liddle

LOVE IN A COLD CLIMATE

When in the bedroom the nitty-gritty
Means that a lady must look pretty.
Swathed in satin, draped in silk,
Smelling of rosebuds dipped in milk.
There's no romance in bedsocks
Or thermolactyl vests,
And it's hard to be seductive
When your chilblains are being pests.
Oh will you love me, love me yet
When wrapped inside my winceyette?

WINDOWS IN WINTER

Why am I here
In this place?
New beginnings
Draw me inside.
Overhead planes,
Where are they going?
Seeking adventure
In some other place?
Now I am grounded;
What am I doing here
In this place?
New beginnings,
Testing my feelings,
Entering inside, and
Reaching the stars.

THOUGHTS

Blank, blank as the page in front of me, my mind;
I cannot find a thing to write about.
My thoughts fly free,
Wheeling and circling,
Swooping close,
But not so close that I can snatch
And capture them.
The idea pleases though.

Words would pinion wings of thought,
Inhibit flight.
Why should I try to tie them to the page
With imagery imperfect, phrases trite?
I'll let them soar
In spheres that have no boundary,
And far beyond.
They will return; they will not die.
For in my mind they hatched,
Stretched fledgling wings
And waited for the strength to fly.
Imprinting at the moment of their birth,
Though they fly free,
Yet still these thoughts belong to me,
Return to earth.

Reflections

A world of wingèd thoughts at my command,
I conjure up whatever suits my mood.
Song thrush trilling, kestrel killing,
Hooded eagle brooding
Over some imagined slight,
While owl sits, ever-watchful,
In the stillness of the night,
And magpie hoards
The shiny trinkets of delight.

So fly, my thoughts, fly free;
Enjoy the freedom of your wings
While, earthbound, your creator savours
All the magic that your freedom brings.

Printed in the United Kingdom
by Lightning Source UK Ltd.
120028UK00001B/58-72